Breads and Biscuits

Library of Congress Cataloging-in-Publication Data

De Villiers, Stoffelina Johanna Adriana.
Breads and biscuits.

(First cookbook library / S.J.A. de Villiers and
E. van der Berg)
Includes index.
Summary: Introduces young chefs to the making of
breads and biscuits.
1. Bread—Juvenile literature. 2. Biscuits—Juvenile
literature. [1. Bread. 2. Biscuits. 3. Cookery]
I. Van der Berg, Eunice. II. Johnson, Marita, ill.
III. Title. IV. Series: De Villiers, Stoffelina Johanna
Adriana. First cookbook library.

TX769.D44 1985 641.8'15 85-12697
ISBN 0-918831-80-6
ISBN 0-918831-35-0 (lib. bdg.)

ISBN 0-918831-35-0 lib. bdg.
ISBN 0-918831-80-6 trade bdg.

Series Editor: MaryLee Knowlton
Cover Illustrations: Renée Graef
Typeset by Superior Printing • Milwaukee, Wisconsin 53223, USA

Breads and Biscuits

S.J.A. de Villiers
and
Eunice van der Berg

Illustrated By
Marita Johnson

Gareth Stevens Publishing
Milwaukee

First Cookbook Library

Getting Ready To Cook
Drinks and Desserts
One Dish Meals
Vegetables and Salads
Breads and Biscuits
Cookies, Cakes, and Candies

These books will show you how easy it is to cook and what fun it is, too.

Everything you have to do is clearly illustrated and the methods you will learn are the same as those used in advanced cookbooks. Once you learn these methods, you will be able to follow recipes you find in any cookbook.

Breads and biscuits go well with any meal. You'll learn recipes for these and muffins too. We'll even teach you how to make pancakes.

If you are concerned about salt, sugar, and fats in your diet, you may reduce the amount called for or substitute other ingredients in many of the recipes. Ask a grown-up for suggestions.

More information about nutrition, ingredients, and cooking methods can be found in GETTING READY TO COOK, a companion volume to this book.

CONTENTS

Black arrows ➡ in some recipes are reminders to ask a grown-up to help you.

Whole-Wheat Bread
(makes one loaf)

Take Out:

small mixing bowl
large mixing bowl
measuring cups
measuring spoons
teaspoon
wooden spoon
bread pan (9″ x 4″)
knife
aluminum foil
oven mitts
cooling rack

What You'll Need

2½ cups whole-wheat flour
½ teaspoon cinnamon
¼ teaspoon salt
2 teaspoons baking powder
1 teaspoon baking soda
1 beaten egg
½ cup molasses
¼ cup brown sugar
¼ cup vegetable oil
1 teaspoon grated lemon or orange peel
⅔ cup yogurt or buttermilk

➡ 1. Grease the bread pan. Preheat the oven to 375°.

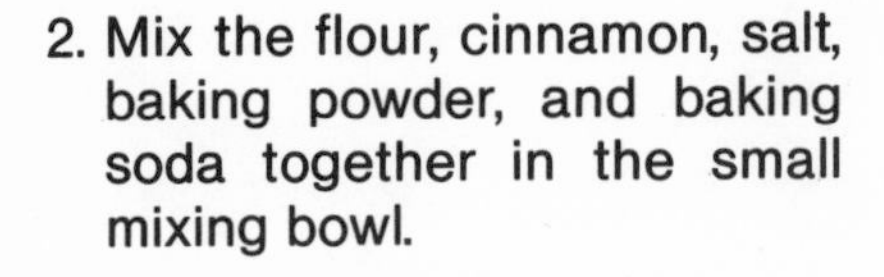

2. Mix the flour, cinnamon, salt, baking powder, and baking soda together in the small mixing bowl.

3. Combine the egg, molasses, brown sugar, vegetable oil, and grated lemon or orange peel in the large mixing bowl.

4. Add the flour mixture to the ingredients in the large mixing bowl.

5. Add the ⅔ cup yogurt or buttermilk to the mixture.

6. Pour the dough into the greased bread pan and level the top with the wooden spoon.

➡ 7. Bake for about 50 minutes.

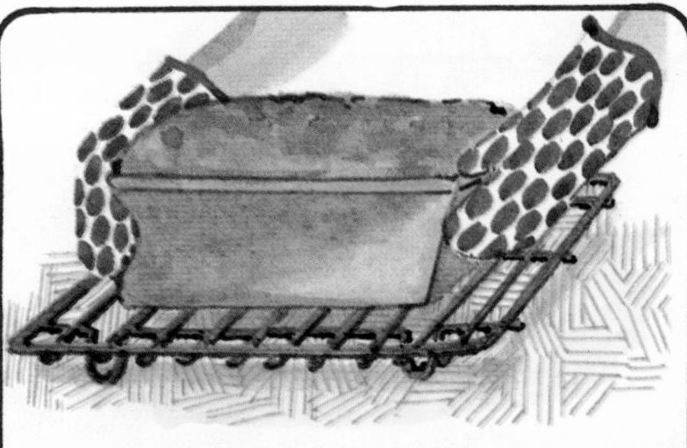

➡ 8. Remove the bread from the oven with the oven mitts. Put it on the cooling rack for 15 minutes. Turn off the oven heat.

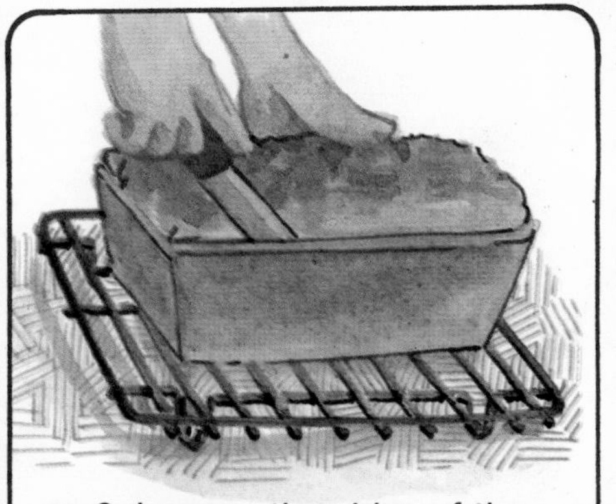

➡ 9. Loosen the sides of the bread with a knife.

➡ 10. Turn it out onto the cooling rack.

11. Slice the bread and serve with butter and jam while it's still warm. Try one of the recipes for special butters on page 31.

Crêpes
(makes 12 crêpes)

Take Out:

2 mixing bowls
measuring spoons
sifter
egg beater
heavy frying pan (6″ diameter)
spatula
tablespoon
saucepan and a dinner plate which will fit on top

What You'll Need

1 cup flour
¼ teaspoon salt
1 cup milk
3 eggs
cinnamon and sugar

1. Sift the flour into a mixing bowl.

2. Beat the eggs, milk, and salt well in the other mixing bowl using the egg beater.

3. Add the flour, three tablespoons at a time, to the egg mixture. Beat until there are no lumps left before adding the next three tablespoons. The batter should be thin enough so that it will spread easily in the hot pan. This will ensure thin crêpes.

➡ 4. Half fill the saucepan with hot water. Put the dinner plate on top. Place the saucepan on one of the back burners at low heat.

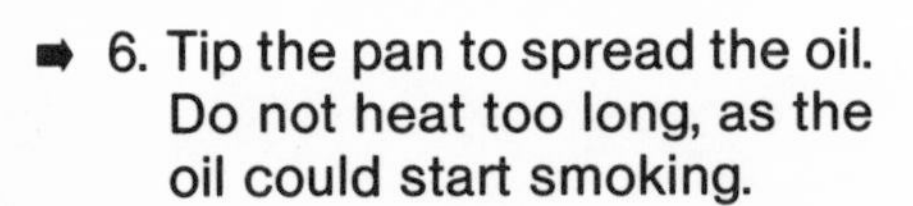

➡ 5. Turn on a burner to high. Pour one teaspoon oil into the pan and place it on the heat.

➡ 6. Tip the pan to spread the oil. Do not heat too long, as the oil could start smoking.

7. Use the ¼ cup measuring cup and nearly fill it with batter. Let the excess batter drip off into the mixing bowl.

➡ 8. Hold the handle of the hot frying pan in one hand. With your other hand, empty the batter from the measuring cup into the middle of the pan.

➡ 9. Tip the pan so that the batter covers the bottom of the pan.

➡ 10. Put the pan back on the heat. As soon as the edges of the crêpe become dry and crisp, it is ready to be turned.

➡ 11. Lift the crêpe carefully with the spatula and turn it over.

➡ 12. Place the crêpe on the dinner plate over hot water to keep it warm.

➡ 13. Cook the other crêpes in the same way until all the batter has been used.

14. Sprinkle cinnamon and sugar over each crêpe and roll it with a fork before serving.

Muffins
(makes 12 muffins)

Take Out:

muffin pan
measuring cups
measuring spoons
mixing bowl
small mixing bowl
sifter
egg beater
2 tablespoons
knife
oven mitts

What You'll Need

1¾ cups flour
2 teaspoons baking powder
¾ teaspoon salt
¼ cup sugar
¾ cup milk
¼ cup melted butter
2 eggs

➡ 1. Preheat the oven to 400°.

2. Grease the muffin cups.

3. Sift the flour, baking powder, and salt into the mixing bowl. Add the sugar.

4. Beat the eggs with the egg beater in the small mixing bowl. Add the butter and milk and beat them all together.

5. Add the egg mixture to the flour mixture.

6. Fold in the egg mixture with the tablespoon until the flour is wet. The batter will be lumpy.

7. Use the two tablespoons to drop some batter into the muffin cups. The muffin cups should be ⅔ full.

➡ 8. Put the muffins immediately into the oven for 20 to 25 minutes.

➡ 9. Use oven mitts to remove the pan from the oven. Turn off the oven heat.

➡ 10. Loosen the sides of the muffins in the cups with the knife. You can serve them in a basket lined with a napkin.

Bran Muffins

(makes 18 muffins)

Take Out:

muffin pan
mixing bowl
small mixing bowl
sifter
egg beater
measuring cups
measuring spoons
tablespoon
cutting board
oven mitts

What You'll Need

1½ cups flour
2 teaspoons baking soda
¼ teaspoon salt
1 cup bran
½ cup sugar
1 cup buttermilk
1 egg
6 tablespoons oil
3 tablespoons molasses

➡ 1. Preheat the oven to 350°.

2. Grease the muffin cups.

3. Sift the flour, baking soda, and salt into the mixing bowl. Stir in the bran.

4. Beat the egg and buttermilk together in the small mixing bowl.

5. Mix the molasses and oil in the measuring cup.

6. Add the molasses mixture to the egg mixture. Stir thoroughly with the tablespoon.

7. Add this to the dry mixture and stir just enough to mix.

8. Spoon the batter into the muffin cups.

➡ 9. Bake for 20 minutes. Remove the muffin pan from the oven with oven mitts. Place it on the cutting board. Turn off the oven heat.

➡ 10. Lift the muffins from the cups with a knife. You can put them into a basket lined with a napkin.

11. Serve the muffins hot with butter and honey.

Breakfast Biscuits

(makes 12 biscuits)

Take Out:

- baking sheet
- cutting board
- sifter
- mixing bowl
- pastry blender
- measuring cups
- measuring spoons
- 2 small mixing bowls
- egg beater
- table knife
- pastry cutter
- spatula
- pastry brush
- oven mitts
- cooling rack

What You'll Need

- flour for the sheet and board
- 1¾ cups flour
- 2¼ teaspoons baking powder
- 1 tablespoon sugar
- ½ teaspoon salt
- ¼ cup butter
- 2 eggs
- ⅓ cup cream

1. Grease the baking sheet. Sift one teaspoon of flour over the whole surface. Sprinkle two tablespoons of flour on the cutting board.

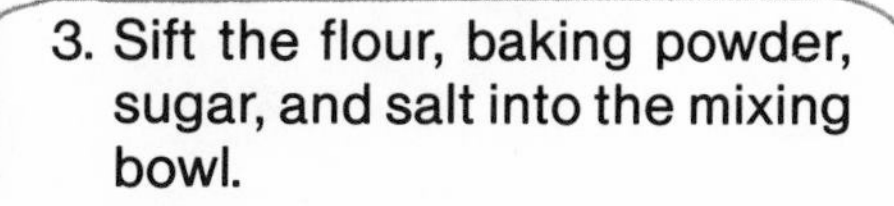

➡ 2. Preheat the oven to 450°.

3. Sift the flour, baking powder, sugar, and salt into the mixing bowl.

4. Rub the butter into the flour with your fingertips or cut it into the flour with the pastry blender until it forms crumbs.

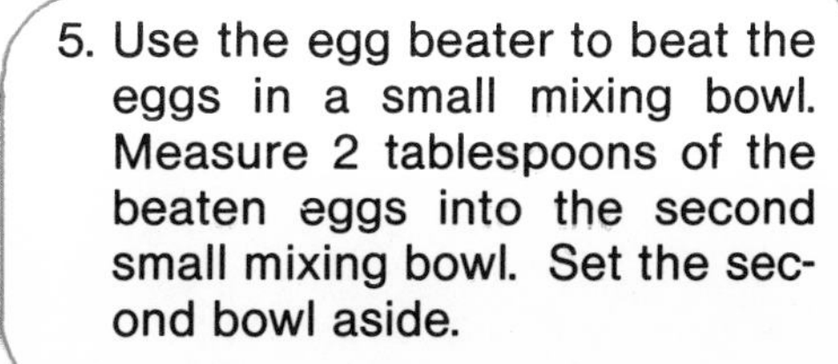

5. Use the egg beater to beat the eggs in a small mixing bowl. Measure 2 tablespoons of the beaten eggs into the second small mixing bowl. Set the second bowl aside.

6. Add the cream to the beaten eggs in the first bowl. Using the egg beater, whip thoroughly. Make a well in the dry ingredients. Pour the egg mixture into it.

7. Cut the egg mixture into the flour mixture with the table knife until it is just wet through. Do not mix any longer.

8. Turn out the dough onto the cutting board. Press it lightly together with your fingers. Handle it as little as possible.

9. Rub the dough from your hands into the empty mixing bowl.

10. Lightly press the dough on the board to a thickness of ¾ inch. Sprinkle more flour on the board if necessary.

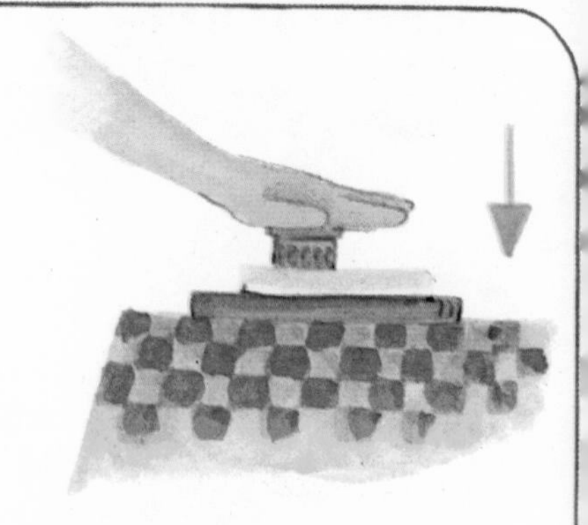

11. Use the pastry cutter to cut round biscuits out of the dough. Press evenly on the pastry cutter when pushing it through the dough.

12. Cut out all the biscuits closely together.

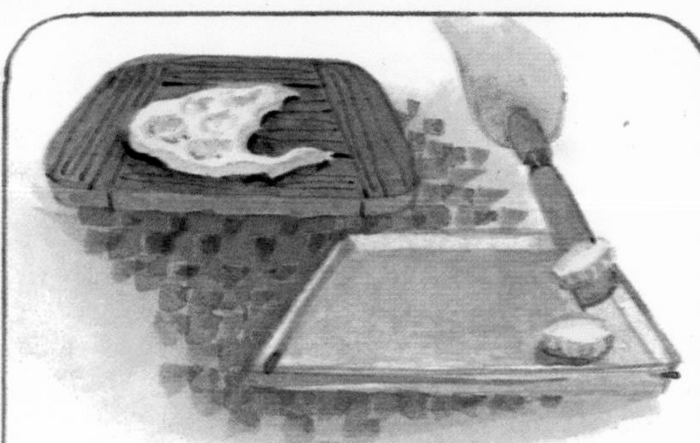

13. Lift them carefully onto the baking sheet with the spatula. Take care not to spoil their shape. Place them ½ inch apart.

14. Press the remaining dough lightly together and cut out more biscuits.

15. Add a pinch of salt to the eggs that were set aside. Use the pastry brush to brush some of this mixture over the top of every biscuit.

➡ 16. Bake the biscuits for 15 minutes in the oven. Remove the baking sheet from the oven with oven mitts and put it on the cooling rack. Turn off the heat.

17. Serve the biscuits hot with butter and jam.

Cheese Muffins
(makes 12 muffins)

Take Out:

muffin pan
large mixing bowl
small mixing bowl
measuring cups
measuring spoons
sifter
pastry blender
egg beater
table knife
2 teaspoons
oven mitts
tablespoon

What You'll Need

1 cup cake flour
¼ teaspoon salt
1½ teaspoons baking powder
1½ tablespoons butter
1 egg
⅓ cup milk
¼ cup grated cheddar cheese

➡ 1. Preheat the oven to 350°. Grease the muffin cups.

2. Sift the flour, salt, and baking powder into the mixing bowl.

3. Rub the butter into the flour mixture with your fingers. It can also be cut with the pastry blender until it looks like bread crumbs.

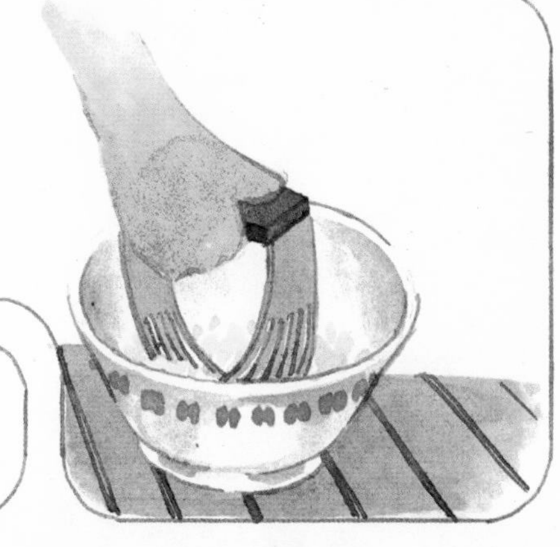

4. Use the egg beater to beat the egg and milk together in the small mixing bowl.

5. Pour the egg mixture onto the flour mixture.

6. Cut it into the flour mixture in all directions with a knife. Do not continue mixing after all the flour is wet.

7. Spread the grated cheese over the mixture and mix it in with a knife. Take care not to mix longer than necessary.

8. Use two teaspoons to drop a little dough into every muffin cup.

➡ 9. Bake the muffins for 20-25 minutes. Remove them from the oven with oven mitts. Turn off the oven heat.

➡ 10. Loosen the muffins by running a knife around the sides. Lift them out with a tablespoon. Serve them hot.

Pancakes
(makes 15 pancakes)

Take Out:

2 mixing bowls
measuring cups
measuring spoons
egg beater
sifter
wooden spoon
tablespoon
spatula
large heavy frying pan
serving dish

What You'll Need

1 egg
3 tablespoons sugar
1¼ cups milk
3 tablespoons oil
1¾ teaspoons baking powder
½ teaspoon salt
1½ cups flour

1. Use an egg beater to beat the egg in a mixing bowl. Add the sugar and beat well.
2. Add half the milk and all the oil to the egg mixture. Beat thoroughly.
3. Sift together the flour, baking powder, and salt into the other mixing bowl.
4. Add the flour mixture gradually to the egg mixture. Stir with a wooden spoon until it is smooth.
5. Stir in the remaining milk slowly until it has blended well.

➡ 6. Turn on the burner to medium heat. Put the serving dish in the oven and turn the heat to low, 250°.

➡ 7. Grease the frying pan with oil and heat it on the burner. You will be making the pancakes three at a time.

➡ 8. Carefully drop three tablespoons of the batter into the hot frying pan. Let each pancake spread in the pan before the next one is dropped next to it. The three pancakes should not touch.

➡ 9. Turn the pancakes carefully with the spatula as soon as bubbles appear on their surfaces. This will take 2-3 minutes.

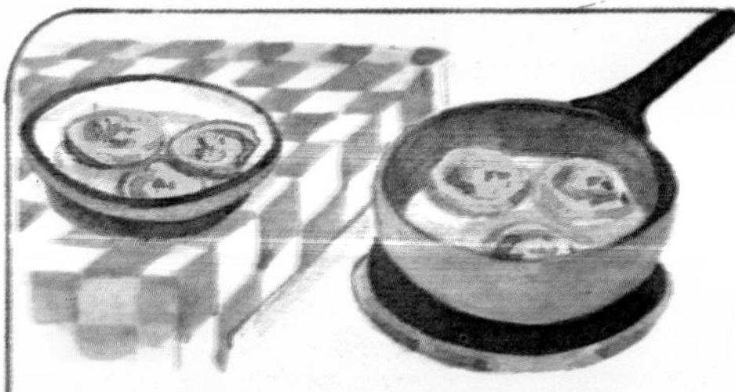

➡ 10. Cook them until they are light brown on both sides. Lift them onto the serving dish.

➡ 11. Keep the pancakes warm in the oven. Repeat the process until all the batter has been used.

12. Serve the pancakes with butter, honey, or syrup.

Raisin Nut Bread
(makes 2 loaves)

Take Out:

2 bread pans (8″x 4″)
saucepan
measuring cups
measuring spoons
sifter
egg beater
wooden spoon
tablespoon
mixing bowl
small mixing bowl
bread knife
cutting board
cooling rack
baking sheet
oven mitts

What You'll Need

1 cup butter
½ cup sugar
1 teaspoon salt
1 cup buttermilk
2 medium eggs
2 cups flour
1½ tablespoons baking powder
3 cups bran
½ cup raisins
½ cup chopped nuts

➡ 1. Preheat the oven to 350°.

2. Grease the bread pans.

➡ 3. Switch on a burner to low heat. Melt the butter in the saucepan on the burner.

➡ 4. Add the sugar, salt, and buttermilk. Stir with the wooden spoon until it has dissolved. Remove the saucepan from the stove and turn off the heat.

5. Allow the melted butter mixture to cool.

6. Beat the eggs in the small mixing bowl. Stir them into the melted butter mixture.

7. Sift together the flour and salt into the mixing bowl. Add the raisins and nuts and blend well with a spoon.

8. Add the melted butter mixture to the flour mixture and stir to blend. Make sure there are no dry patches at the bottom of the mixing bowl.

9. Put the dough into the bread pans. Level off the tops with a spoon.

➡ 10. Bake for one hour. Take the pans out of the oven using the oven mitts. Turn off the oven heat.

➡ 11. Let the loaves cool slightly. Cut them into thick slices with the bread knife.

Honey Muffin
(8 servings)

Take Out:

pie plate (9″ in diameter)
large mixing bowl
small mixing bowl
measuring cups
measuring spoons
sifter
egg beater
small saucepan
wooden spoon
plastic scraper
oven mitts
cooling rack

What You'll Need

1 cup flour
½ cup sugar
1 heaping tablespoon baking powder
¼ teaspoon salt
½ cup milk
3 tablespoons butter
1 egg
4 tablespoons honey
2 tablespoons butter

➡ 1. Preheat the oven to 350°.

2. Grease the pie plate.

3. Sift together the flour, sugar, baking powder, and salt into the large mixing bowl.

➡ 4. Pour the milk into the saucepan and add the butter. Put the saucepan on the burner and turn the heat to medium. Remove the saucepan from the heat as soon as the butter has melted.

5. Beat the egg in the small mixing bowl with the egg beater. Stir it into the milk mixture with the wooden spoon.

6. Stir the lukewarm milk mixture rapidly into the flour mixture until it is smooth. Do not let it stand.

7. Turn the batter immediately into the pie plate. Scrape the mixing bowl with the plastic scraper.

➡ 8. Bake it immediately for 15 minutes.

9. While the muffin is in the oven, clean out the saucepan. Measure out the honey and butter into the saucepan.

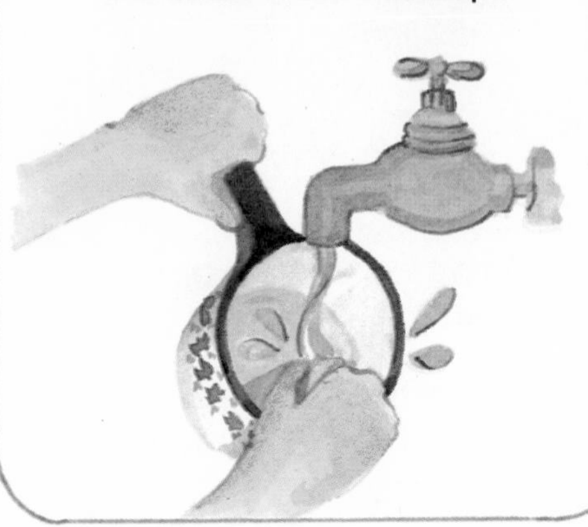

➡ 10. Over low heat, melt the honey and butter. Turn off the heat.

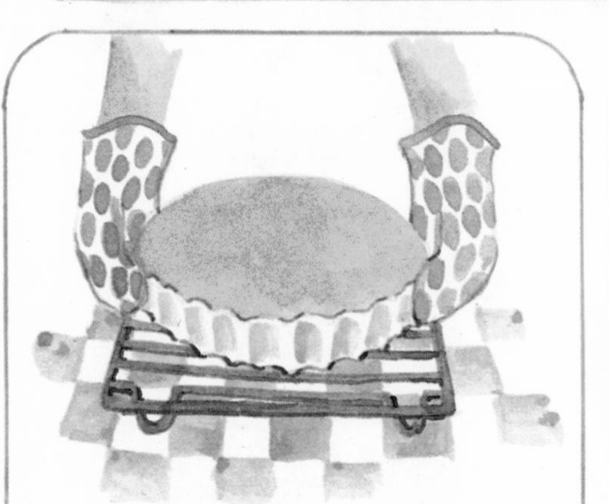

➡ 11. Remove the honey muffin from the oven with the oven mitts and place it on the cooling rack. Turn off the oven heat.

➡ 12. Pour the melted honey and butter mixture over the entire surface of the muffin while it is still hot.

Special Butters

Butters for your biscuits and muffins

Cinnamon Butter

Cream these ingredients together in a mixing bowl:

3 tablespoons soft butter
⅓ cup powdered sugar
1 teaspoon cinnamon

Place the cinnamon butter in the refrigerator for one hour. Serve it on biscuits or muffins.

Honey and Cream Butter

Beat these ingredients together in a mixing bowl:

¼ cup honey
2 tablespoons soft butter
2 tablespoons whipping cream

Chill well and serve it on hot biscuits or muffins.

INDEX

Black arrows ➡ in some recipes are reminders to ask a grown-up to help you.